SMUDGING FOR BEGINNERS

SECRETS FROM A PROFESSIONAL

LEEZA DONATELLA

Printed in the United States of America

First Edition – October 2015

Paperback
ISBN-13: 978-0-9911007-4-3
ISBN-10: 0991100743

Higher Roads Productions
Copyright © 2015

DEDICATION

To friends Ingrid, Melissa and Shell,
whose love and wisdom have guided
me over the years.

And to my sister Toni Ann,
who always believes in me.

CONTENTS

ABOUT THE AUTHOR

LeeZa lives a pretty amazing life, filled with extraordinary experiences and synchronicity. She's trekked through the Amazon in Peru, climbed atop Machu Picchu in the Andes, has been invited to join Shamans in Ayahuasca ceremonies, meditated in the middle of Brazil while, helping charitable organizations, danced on the Great Wall of China and performed Tai Chi with seniors in a small Chinese village where no language was required.

"I've never felt more alive as I strive to help people move forward. The incredible part of traveling around the world is that I've picked up tidbits from the practices of many cultures that I'm now sharing with all of you."

Today she speaks to both U.S. and International audiences about what inspires and motivates us, causes us stress and about using energy to our best advantage to balance, release and heal. The philosophy

LeeZa teaches is about getting to and maintaining the state she calls *"Being Love."*

LeeZa has been working with Energy for decades and is experienced in several modalities: Bio-Energy, Japanese Reiki (a 5 time Reiki Master), Chakra Balancing and Harmonization, Shamanic practices and Emotional Freedom Technique (EFT Tapping).

"I wish you all the LOVE in the Universe. Open your heart to let it in, sigh and breathe the sweet fragrance of the deliciousness of life."
LeeZa Donatella

www.leezadonatella.com

Enjoy LeeZa's newest book,
available on Amazon

The State of Being Love,
Steps to Raise your Vibration
for a Joy Filled Life

PRELUDE

I was first introduced to smudging back in the 1990's, when I left the East Coast and moved to Arizona.

It was at a time when I was ready for the next level, "the bam" that famous chefs refer to when they want to kick the flavor up a notch, when they're cooking. You could say that the people I met and what I experienced helped move me up the spiritual ladder a rung or two.

I had already been channeling since I was 4 years old, working with bio-energy for several years and had a couple of spiritual quests outside the country, immersing myself in an area for several months at a time.

I was inspired to write this book after the many emails I've received based on my online article about smudging, to help those who are experiencing more, especially now with the shift of the planet's energies.

I want to emphasize that your experiences are all tied to your belief system, and that from moment to moment your beliefs can change. My hope is that this book will provide you with the tools so you can cleanse and clear any energy that does not resonate with your higher self or purpose, and help dispel any fears you may have about the energy you're experiencing in your space and person.

After all, it's all just energy. There's absolutely nothing to be afraid of. It's that fear and that negativity, that's keeping you from moving forward.

1
INTRODUCTION

Today smudging has become a mainstream word, with smudge sticks sold in convenience stores and trendy whole food markets. Anyone can light a smudge stick and wave it around. What's lacking is a true understanding and education about harnessing the energy to perform the ceremony to cleanse person, place and object that you'll find in this book.

Some people are intimidated when it comes to anything new. And smudging can sound a bit weird, especially since it's misinterpretation by Hollywood and certain others. At first it can look strange and the majority of people who see it for the first time are taken aback. Well, don't be because it's not complicated. Actually it's been used for millennium, in some form by most cultures throughout history. It's totally safe, so don't worry that you'll invite in less than desirable energy if you do something wrong. In the grand scheme of things, everything is based on intention. And with good intentions and a high state of being, the results are always positive.

I've been using this ancient form of cleansing for decades, and have had wonderful success in my own homes, businesses and person as well as when working with clients.

This book will walk you through a complete cleansing ceremony from beginning to end, as well as provide you with a quick ceremony for everyday cleansing. It contains facts on all the tools involved and goes into detail about the significance of why each tool is chosen and when to use it. It includes specifics about timings and reasons why elements were used by certain cultures.

It also contains descriptions of the energies that are becoming more recognizable to the general public, which may be a reason why you've researched smudging and why I've also added explanations based on decades of experience.

This is not just an ordinary book about how to cleanse a person or place, but a peek into the more esoteric world that's been off limits to the masses for centuries.

For some, this will be eye opening, for others validation of what you're experiencing.

Within these pages is material not normally available to the general public, including what to do should you encounter energetic spirits, and how to get unwanted energy to leave you in peace.

The universe has always had an interesting way of making things happen for me. It seems like when I'm ready to move to the next level, somehow I'm presented with the next piece of the puzzle that assists in my next assignment. I guess that's the way it's supposed to work since Earth *is* a classroom.

I'm also assuming that you've found this book, not just because you're interested in smudging, but that you're ready to transcend into a higher vibration, one that will have you evaluating and seeing life differently, as you experience more of what's behind the veil.

2

REASONS TO SMUDGE TODAY

Smudging cleanses the energy in the locations, objects and the energetic fields of persons, ridding them of residual or lower vibrational frequencies/energetic imprints. I think it's important to emphasize that **energy is just emotion in motion,** as I provide specific reasons why people are smudging today.

See the *Best Times to Smudge* chapter for the absolute best timing for smudging depending on the reason. Below are a few reasons why people are smudging today.

FOR CLEANSING OBJECTS

There will be times when you have an object you want to cleanse. For example, perhaps you received a gift from someone with whom you are no longer in a relationship with. Instead of discarding the item, you could just cleanse it, releasing the object's attachment to that person.

Often a piece of inherited jewelry retains the energy of the person who was wearing it. Maybe you just picked up some eclectic item at a garage sale. These are perfect items to cleanse by smudging to remove the energy of their last owner from that object. See the instructions for cleansing an object, located in the **Smudging/Cleansing Ceremonies** chapter.

FOR CLEANSING LOCATIONS

Below are reasons why you would want to cleanse a location:

To Raise Consciousness

The smoke from smudging raises the frequency of a location. I recommend performing a *Quick Smudge* when the energy in your space feels off, as smudging will help restore balance in the home.

After Guests

Ever have a negative Nancy visit your home? Perhaps it's a visit from that mother-in-law of yours who keeps criticizing your cooking or how you raise your children. This is another great time to perform a *Quick Smudge* after they exit your home.

Moving into a New Place of Residence
It doesn't matter if you own the home, if it's a newly built home or if you're renting an apartment or condominium. This is a good time for you to perform a *Complete Location Blessing/Cleansing* of your residence. You'll want to cleanse your space within 1 moon cycle (30 days) of moving in after unpacking. I always advise at least a *Quick Smudge* before you first sleep in the home, if you're able, then performing a *Complete House Blessing/Cleansing* when you've completely unpacked.

Spring Cleaning
I suggest that you always perform a *Complete House Blessing/Cleansing* every spring as part of my spring cleaning, inviting new beginnings along with the fresh lively energy. Actually performing a *Complete House Blessing/Cleansing* at least once every season is a way to keep your home's energy vibrating higher.

Adding New Members to your Household

When someone new moves into your home to live with current members, like through marriage, smudging their belongings will assist in removing the energy they've carried with them from their prior home. This is a perfect time for a *Quick Smudge* of both their belongings as well as the residence.

Major Life Events

A major home improvement project is when the energy of the residence has undergone some alteration. So many times I get emails after someone does a major remodel stating that there never had anything **odd** happen before the remodel, but now, they're experiencing something a little strange.

Other life events include natural disasters, like a hurricane or tornado, times when there's a huge energy upheaval and disturbance.

Perhaps you've had a life changing event, like losing your job, having a child or received bad news about a health condition.

A *Quick Smudge* of the residence at that time is recommended.

Removing the Energy of a Loved One

We all have ended relationships, had roommates leave or lost someone we love, even a family pet. It doesn't mean that the person was negative in anyway, but this is another good time to cleanse the space and remove the energies of the person that is no longer living in that space. It's not that you are disrespecting them in anyway by doing so, but it will help you move forward, which is of course what they would want you to do. I recommend a *Complete House Blessing/ Cleansing* to rid the space of their residual energy.

Removing Unwanted Energetic Spirits

Not everyone experiences this, but I would be lying if I told you that all locations do not hold energy, they do. Whether you're sensitive and experience them as something very obvious, like seeing a shadow out of the corner of your eye, have something continually moved that cannot be blamed on the family dog, hear new sounds that are not common to your home or area, or perhaps even feel or smell something, then it's time for a *Complete House Blessing/Cleansing* to rid the space of residual energy. There's never anything to be afraid of here, remember that it's just energy.

FOR CLEANSING PEOPLE

Now that we've touched on reasons to cleanse your location, let me give you a few reasons why you would want to cleanse people.

To Raise Consciousness

There are outer worldly reasons to use smoke. The smoke aids in enhancing one's state of consciousness. For centuries it's been used to raise the vibrational frequency of the person and invite spiritual connections. I use smoke when working with clients to help them move toward that state I call "Being Love."

Adding New Members to your Household

Like discussed previously with belongings,

when someone new moves into your home to live with current members, a *Quick Smudge* can be used as a way of welcoming them into your home and help assimilate their energy into the new environment. It also removes the energy they brought with them from their prior place of residence.

Lowered Energy in the Home
Smudging is particularly helpful during times of stress, after arguments with people in the household or on the phone with someone. It's always a good idea to perform a *Quick Smudge* if you're feeling negative, sad, depressed or anxious.

After Being in Lower Vibrational Places
Okay, so you may have just come from a business meeting where everyone was arguing over the next big thing, frustrated coming off a packed train, plane, or returning home after being stuck in traffic as part of your daily commute. Perhaps you were just at someone's home and you noticed that there's something different about yourself, you can't pinpoint what it is, but

you're irritated, or just not your usual self. Something's going on and you just feel off in some way. Depending on your vibration and state of being, the people or places you just visited have effected the energy that surrounds you, also called your energetic field. Remember that energy is *emotion in motion* and depending on several factors it can penetrate this field, and stay with you. Many people pick up the energy from their surroundings and it's very noticeable to them and the people in their life that something's just not right. When you stay in the *"Being Love"* state, you're vibrating so high that nothing can effect your vibration. For people who have not yet achieved that state, a *Quick Smudge* is a way to help equalize and raise you up.

After Interacting with Lower Vibrational People

I don't consider people inherently bad, although I will admit that there are people who just don't understand that it's better to *Be Love* than anything else. Since love has the highest vibration, people who live in less than Love are energetically vibrating lower.

Perhaps you just got off the phone with one of *those* people. I'm referring to the person who has a lower vibrational frequency, let's call them the Debbie Downer, the Complainer, or the Poor Me; we all know at least one. It's that person that when we see them come up on our caller ID, we have to determine if we take the call, knowing that we'll be on the phone with them for over an hour and after the call finally ends, we feel exhausted. That's because we allow their vibration to effect our vibration, not knowing how to prevent it from happening. A *Quick Smudge* will definitely get your energy level high once again.

Removing Energetic Attachments
Living People
Have you ever broken up with someone and somehow you still feel them. They may not have mistreated you, or perhaps they did. Either way, you're no longer together, but they may still invade your dreams and

thoughts, even though that's the last thing that you want!

Some theorists call this cording, tentacles or hooks because they believe that the other person is still attached to your energetic field. I think of it a little differently, so let me give you an example: I have an old friend who lives on the other side of the country. I don't get to speak to her much, maybe once or twice a year, but all of a sudden thoughts of her pop into my head and 2 minutes later the phone rings, and it's her on the other end. If another person is thinking of you they're unknowingly sending you energetic vibes. Unlike an old friend, in the case of an old partner, it's energy that you may not want in your space.

In my world, I just call it getting a fresh start and that's why I suggest this as a good time for a *Quick Smudge* of oneself, to cleanse your energetic field.

Non-Living
There are people who give themselves up

willingly and allow their physical and energetic bodies to be used by entities to help others. Such is the case with famous channels who make an agreement with external energies for the greater good. I've met several of these people in my spiritual travels in the U.S. and abroad. I believe that the same can be said when we experience *grace* as we're filled with the spirit. At times in my life I have experienced such grace in my energetic field that I smelled roses when none were present, and felt uplifted and light as if I were floating so filled with love that my heart was overflowing, an energy that's pure love.

What causes us concern is not what I refer to above, but lower vibrational energies that can invade someone's energetic body without their knowledge or permission. I don't have a ton of experience in this area, nor do I want to, but have been informed about such things from people who I respect. It's been communicated that an energetic body attachment can be hard to discern and I don't want to get into too much detail here, but smudging can assist in balancing that person's energy. If you really feel as if you've an experienced an energetic attachment like I'm describing, it's a good idea to speak to someone who specializes in those types of situations.

Frequently Asked Questions about Reasons to Smudge

I was looking into smudging my house, however, I haven't noticed any negative spirits or spiritual energy. My reason for smudging would be to cleanse my house of the negative energy from arguments and fights that have taken place. Would smudging be okay in that circumstance?

Answer: That's absolutely a good time to smudge, to return balance and love to your home.

3

COMPLETE SMUDGING/ CLEANSING TOOL KIT

After decades of performing cleansings, I use materials that I believe have specific significance. Below are the tools you'll need to perform a full cleansing ceremony and the materials for your own smudging tool kit:

- A smudge stick:
  I use white sage when smudging a person and cleansing homes and businesses. Sage is used to safeguard, protect and defend as it eliminates negative energies.

- Something to hold the Ash:
  As you're moving around a person or location you'll want to have something to catch the ash of the burning smudge stick. I follow Native and Shamanic practices and use an abalone shell. I use green abalone since green signifies healing.

- Something to light the Smudge Stick:
  You can use small charcoal briquettes
  specifically used for burning herb or
  resins, matches, a lighter or a candle to
  light and keep the smudging material
  burning.

- A wand or feather:
  You'll want to have something to fan the
  smoke. I like to use a feather wrapped
  in a natural material, like leather.
  Native American tribes use eagle or
  turkey feathers wrapped in the skins of
  animals like deer, moose and other
  creatures.
  Note: You never want to blow on a
  smudge stick to keep it burning, because
  in Native American cultures it signifies
  giving away your strength.

- Salt:
  Sprinkle salt in the center of a room and
  around the outside walls and doorways
  of your home as a powerful absorber of
  energy. Salt also helps with purification.
  I only use Himalayan pink salt because

pink symbolized unconditional love and this salt comes from the great Salt Range of the Himalayas, an area estimated to be about 800 million years old. The energy vibration of this salt amplifies vibrational frequency and helps bridge the gap between our physical, mental and spiritual selves.

- Anointing Oils:
  Not enough people are educated about anointing oils and it's really a shame, because it's such a good practice that's been used for centuries in cleansing, purification and protection ceremonies and rituals. The oils I use for anointing come from a blend of Sandalwood, Frankincense, Myrrh and Rose essentials. I talk about their spiritual significance in a later chapter.

WHERE TO FIND THE BEST SUPPLIES

You can create your own anointing oils by using organic essential oils. Places to try and find oils and smudge sticks also include local

New Age bookstores and shops, as well as some organic farmers markets.

Frequently Asked Questions about Materials

Below are some of the frequently asked questions I've received from readers about materials.

Can I reuse a smudge stick?
Answer: Absolutely, there's no reason why you can't use a smudge stick more than once, so go ahead and use it again.

I met a man in town when I was living in Sedona, AZ. He was toting a dozen huge smudge sticks that he had just purchased from a local New Age shop. I looked at him and jokingly asked, "Are you smudging Windsor Castle?"

"Oh, no," he replied. The lady in the store told me that they were only good for one use."

I really get frustrated when I hear about charlatans telling people other than the truth for their own personal gain, like selling more products or services. I'm glad you found this book so I can help dispel some mistruths.

How many times can I reuse a smudge stick?
Answer: Until you can no longer hold it comfortably without getting burned.

Can more than one person smudge?
Answer: Absolutely. My friend Michele of Healing Spirit of Sedona and I have joined forces to smudge a place together, especially when there's an energy disturbance.

I bought a 3 pack of the smaller sticks. If one gets low during my smudging can I light a new one?
Answer: Yes, it's all about intention. If you light the new stick and continue with the blessing and accept the new smoke, then you're in good shape.

I got a large smudge stick to bless and cleanse a friend's vacation home. Should I use it here at my home first or can't you reuse it in different homes?

Answer: Again, it's all about intention. I bring my own smudge sticks to the places that I cleanse, including my friend's places. It doesn't matter how many places that you use them, just put your intention into the home before using the stick each time.

Can I put the sage on a metal alter dish and go around the room with it?

Answer: Yes. When I provide information on materials I'm giving you my recommendations based on decades of experience, but there's never a wrong answer when intention is of the highest good.

I began smudging but the smudge stick wouldn't stay lit. I was able to do all of my upstairs and a couple of rooms on my main floor but couldn't finish the main floor or the basement. Was the smudging I did a waste of time? Will the negativity just be able to move elsewhere within the home?

Answer: Just know that smudging is never wasted, no matter if you complete it or not. However, I will tell you that it's better to replenish the materials that you need as soon as you are able and to smudge the entire space again.

What do I do if my smudge stick goes out?
Answer: All smudge sticks are not created equally or wrapped the same or use the same material. You can relight them, there's nothing wrong with doing that.

What if I can't find sage and desperately need to smudge. What do I do?
Answer: Although I prefer and typically use white sage to smudge, if I'm in a place where I absolutely can't find any, and need to smudge, then I use what's available. At times I've even tied a few incense sticks together and used them to make one. In a pinch when I'm in the woods and have nothing with me, I gather grasses and braid them together.

Remember, it's all about intention my dears!

4

A Bit of Smudging History

Okay, so I know that you all want to get into the detail about smudging, but to get a full appreciation of smudging I feel that it's necessary to share a few definitions and education about the history of this cleansing ceremony, for I know that it will assist you as you perform this ancient ritual.

What Smudging is Not

Smudging is a cleansing and **not** a form of Witchcraft, Black Magic, Voodoo or Evil. If anyone tries to convince you that this is the case, then point them to one of the many traditional uses of smudging used today around the world. Here's a perfect example: In some Christian religions, if you've ever gone to church around Easter, you know the smell I'm referring to. They're actually burning a few types of Frankincense (1 of the 3 gifts of the Magi) in their ceremony as they move up and down the aisles waving it back and forth. This action provides cleansing and purification and has been used in Christian religions dating back to Christianity earliest days. It still plays an important role in the Catholic Mass, showing honor and respect, inviting purity, and representing virtue as the ritual's intent is to be a vehicle to send prayers toward God.

Thank goodness we're not living in the time of quick judgement like when people were burned at the stake.

Today people widely accept smudging as a way to purify and cleanse the energies associated with a space, object or person.

ORIGINAL MEANING OF THE WORD SMUDGE
Cleansing and purification rituals have been performed for centuries, but the word *smudge* was actually first used to describe the specific tool, a sacred smoke bowl that was used by Native Americans in their ceremonies, dating back before the Aztecs. It's been a part of many Native cultures, particularly by tribes in the Americas that include Shamanic practices.

Although this book provides details about the cleansing ritual called smudging, I wanted you to know that there's a lot more going on here with the many different materials over history that have been used in ceremonies to communicate with the spirit world. So even though the word smudging has become popular, the rituals and ceremonies that have been used for eons are all doing the same thing; cleansing!

For example, did you know that the smoke of sacred plants has been used in some way in every culture throughout history as a way to get closer to and communicate with the Gods?

Smoke has also been used for spiritual rites of passage like vision quests and spirit communications.

I was not surprised to discover ancient Egyptian hieroglyphs depicting Pharaoh's using smoke to raise their vibration in ritual ceremonies to assist in the communication with the Gods. The Pharaoh Ramesses even burned incense as a ritual offering.

5

THE SPIRITUAL SIGNIFICANCE OF MATERIALS

WHAT HERBS, RESINS AND OILS SHOULD I USE?

I get asked a lot about other materials used in ceremony and all I have to say is that the choices of what to use for cleansing and protecting are as different as the ceremonies themselves. I happen to use both white sage and an anointing oil when I'm smudging and cleansing homes and persons. These are the ones I list in *The Complete Cleansing Tool Kit* chapter of this book as my staple items.

Below is information on commonly used herbs, plants and resins and their spiritual and energetic significance:

- Cedar (*Thuja*): Used in Native ceremonies, it represents the harmony between the Earthly and the Spiritual planes.

- Frankincense (*Boswellia*): The resin of many of this genius' family trees are used in incense for ceremonial and cleansing purposes and aid in strength and protection.

- Juniper (*Cupressaceae*): Coming from the cypress family, it's believed to purify and create safety.

- Lavender (*Lavandula*): This genius has many types of fragrant varieties. In smudging it's best known to restore balance and a peaceful atmosphere as it attracts loving energy and spirits.

- Mugwort (*Artemisia vulgaris*): An aromatic plant, it's used in ceremonies to stimulate psychic awareness and promote prophetic dreams.

- Myrrh (*Commiphora myrrha*): The resin commonly harvested from this tree species helps raise vibrational frequency.

- Osha Root (*Ligusticum porter*): A medicinal herb used in Native American and Mexican cultures, it's also known to provide protection from negative thoughts and promote mystical dreams.

- Palo Santo (*Bursera graveolens*): Known as a mystical tree, it's related to Frankincense, Myrrh and Copal and is known for its grounding properties as it raises vibrational frequency for deeper connections to Source.

- Pine (Pinus): A conifer tree, known for healing and protection.

- Rose (*Rosaceae*): The petals of the flowers are expressed in the form of an oil. Rose signifies unconditional love and purity.

- Rosemary (*Rosmarinus officinalis*): This powerful healing herb is known to bring clarity to problems. Please take care when using Rosemary if you're pregnant, since it is an emmenagogue (induces menses).

- Sage (*Salvia*): This is the most common sacred material used in Native American rituals and known best for driving out lower vibrational energy, negative emotions and thoughts. It's become more mainstream in western culture and is most commonly used in the smudging ceremonies that we're now all familiar with. I believe that the word sage comes from the Latin root salvare, which means to save, rescue, safeguard, protect and defend. When most people use it in ceremony, it's usually bundled and tied into what is called a smudge stick, but I've been invited to Native ceremonies where loose sage is collected and burned in shells.

- Sagebrush (*Artemisia californica*): Confused with the sage used in most smudge sticks, this is not culinary sage but sagebrush, known to transform energy and bring change.

- Sandalwood (*Santalum*): It's a sacred tree that grows in southern India. It has a lot of spiritual significance and is used to cleanse both place and person of negativity.

- Sweet Grass (*Hierochloe odorata*): Referred to as holy grass, it has an undeniable sweet aroma and is usually braided together and generally used in ceremonies to give thanks and show gratitude. Spiritualists and Native Americans traditionally use it in preparation or initialization of a ritual or healing session. Some use sweet grass to summon positive spirits after sage is used to cleanse, but I don't do that because when I smudge and cleanse a space, I ask that all energy is transmute to Love, the energy with the highest most pure vibration.

- Tobacco (*Nicotiana*): It represents the balance between the yin and yang, of all that is positive and negative.

- Yerba Santa (*Eriodictyon californicum*): This plant is used in ceremonies to set and protect boundaries.

TIMES WHEN YOU CAN'T BURN MATERIALS
Using oils and sage in my practice, there have been occasions where I'm unable to burn sage as part of a cleansing ceremony. This is when I rely on the use of oils and sprays in my tool kit. I always have a "Smudging Spray" made from a few organic essential oils from the above list, diluted in water in my arsenal, in case I need to smudge without flame. The high note in that mixture is of course Sage oil. I use that along with my Himalayan salt to work through the location and use the anointing oil on the persons in that locale.

Materials used by Ceremony Type
In addition to smudging ceremonies, below is a list of other rituals and materials used by other cultures.

Medicine Wheel

As you would guess, the Medicine Wheel is actually a circle that is used by Native American tribes in purification ceremonies, separated into 4 sections, each with their corresponding sacred plant.

- North - Sage
- South – Sweetgrass
- East - Tabacco
- West – Cedar

These plants are used like medicine when smudging the person to be purified. They are ground then burned in an abalone shell then fanned with either an eagle or turkey feather as the person uses their hands to take in the smoke. I've participated in the creation and use of medicine wheels while living the American southwest. It is a time lost tradition that you can revive if you choose, creating a large circle outlined by stones, with more detailed instructions on ceremonies on the Web.

Ancient Cultures of the East

Both frankincense and myrrh have been

used for thousands of years by ancient civilizations in Babylonia and Egypt, burning them during religious ceremonies as they cleansed and connected to the Gods.

References in the Hebrew Bible point to their use in the sacred temples in Jerusalem with some Christian religions still using frankincense in their celebrations.

Frankincense and Myrrh were 2 of the Gifts of the 3 Wise Men (Gold, Frankincense and Myrrh) that were delivered to the infant upon his birth.

Palo Santo has traditional uses in South American ceremonies.

Many Shamans in Peru's spiritual communities create a traditional Agua de Florida (flower water) to use in their healing ceremonies which includes Rose, a flower with one of the highest vibrations.

6

WHAT IS VIBRATIONAL FREQUENCY?

I added this chapter for those who are not familiar with vibrational frequencies. Let me use the tuning fork, the device that produces a harmonic vibration as an example.

When its two prongs are struck, the sound can be heard as well as the vibration physically felt by most people. Now think of your body as a large tuning fork. All the atoms in your cells vibrate at a particular rate or frequency. Can you visualize this? Good, because this is just science boys and girls.

Now take a look at a set of tuning forks. They all look the same, but when you strike them they don't sound the same, nor does it feel or resonate the same within you. You may actually feel them in different parts of your body, and you should, but I'll leave that for another book.

Now this is where the definition gets expansive. Each emotion has its own frequency. That may be a lot to grasp so let me educate you about a book by David R. Hawkins called *Transcending the Levels of Consciousness*. David assigned a number to the vibratory level of main emotions, putting them on a scale from 20 to 1000. At the bottom of the scale are emotions like shame and guilt and at the top of the scale are love, joy, peace and enlightenment. It's suggested that most of the population's energetic field is vibrating no higher than 150.

The higher your vibration, the closer you get to vibrating enlightenment like the Masters: Jesus, Buddha, etc. Pretty good company, don't you think?

This scale can confuse people, so in my book, **The State of Being Love**, I made it simple. You can either be in that state I refer to as "Being Love," or your vibrating "Something Else."

You vibrate higher while *Being Love,* which includes unconditional love for every person and situation regardless of the perceived outcome, viewing each experience as a gift. Vibrating *Something Else* on the other hand includes every other emotion (what most term negativity) including but not limited to shame, guilt, despair, worry, envy, jealously, control, judgement, anger, hatred, doubt, sadness, righteousness, etc.

When our emotions (*energy in motion*) are in that higher vibrational range, something inside us changes. And when we change, our world and reality shifts to something that is so delicious, words hardly describe it. An added benefit of you vibrating higher is something I have personally experienced, quicker rejuvenation. I first noticed this benefit after a friend commented on a photo on my PC, stating that they didn't know I was in Peru last year. I laughed, stating that the photo was over 20 years old and I had the local shop scan it to my PC. I was ecstatic when I discovered my own personal correlation to vibrating higher and a sort of fountain of youth.

So what does vibrational frequency have to do with smudging?

Smudging helps remove lower vibrational frequencies and energies from your space and energetic field, leaving only higher vibrations, like peace, joy and love in their place.

That's why we feel so good after we smudge. We have cleaned up that energy, allowing more positive experiences to come our way. Now if we could just stay in a loving place emotionally all the time, it surely would be heaven on Earth.

7

PREPARING THE LOCATION FOR SMUDGING

If you're performing a *Complete Location Blessing/Cleansing*, then you want to follow a few steps that will make it easier to move about as you put the space in the best possible condition to smudge.

- The first thing I always suggest to people is to clean the entire home. Put all those dirty dishes in the dishwasher, wipe down the countertops, wash the bed linens and vacuum. Use common sense and don't leave food out since you'll be waving a smoking smudge stick around. Just think of it as if you were having your out-of-town relatives over and you want to ensure your place looks its best.

- Adjust your furniture allowing you to easily move around your home.

- Open all the shades and curtains on all windows.

- Open all doors including the closets.

- Open the cabinets.

I also suggest that you open the windows a comfortable amount, using common sense if you live in a climate where the outside temperature is below zero.

8

PREPARING THE SMUDGING FACILITATOR

So you'll be the one performing the smudging or perhaps you've hired a professional to come in and cleanse your home, family or business. When I perform a smudging ceremony, I take a few steps to get ready so I am the best channel of loving energy. You'll want to take about 20-30 minutes to prepare yourself before beginning the work. You be the judge about what works best for you.

I take a little longer, since I deal with a lot of energy in the locations where I work. The joke is that I'm like Norm from Cheers, it seems all the spirits know my name.

MEDITATE, GROUND AND CENTER

First I find a quiet place where I will not be distracted. I draw the blinds, light a candle and burn some incense. I sit there and meditate, usually for 20-30 minutes until I am at peace, finding balance and center. Not everyone has already established that discipline, so for those who are not familiar with meditation practices, I suggest that you pull out a meditation CD or find one on YouTube. I've been threatening to create a guided meditation for a smudging ceremony including preparation, so perhaps it will be available on the web by the time you read this book. If not, below are a few words of guidance. Remember, there's no wrong way to meditate. Whatever you experience is right.

Begin by closing your eyes. Relax and focus on your breath, feeling the air entering your nostrils, flowing into your lungs, then slowly out your nose again. Just breathe naturally as you notice your body beginning to relax.

Slowly roll your shoulders forward and then slowly back again. Then lean your head from side to side, lowering your left ear toward your left shoulder and then your right ear toward your right shoulder.

Move your focus on the areas of your body one at a time as they begin to relax. If you get distracted, don't worry, everyone does, even the Masters. Just return your focus to your breathing, paying attention to the area from the bridge of your nose to the opening of your nostrils, as you feel the air entering and exiting.

Once you feel relaxed, you'll want to ground yourself. You can do this by focusing on your First Chakra, which is located at the base of your spine. Imagine that strong roots, like those from an oak tree, are winding down from the base of your spine into the Earth. They root you to the planet and keep you grounded, helping you gain balance and center.

Now bring your attention to your Crown Chakra, located at the top of your head. Imagine that it's the most beautiful pink rose you've ever seen. With petals up, they each slowly open as you feel your crown opening, receiving loving energy from all around you.

After you're at peace, then you'll anoint yourself using the instructions in the

Anointing Yourself section of the ***Anointing Oils*** chapter of this book.

9

ANOINTING OILS

WHY USE OILS

History

I first was introduced to anointing oils when I was in Peru back in the 1990's. It was in South America where I first had a true appreciation of the symbolic references that seem to cross over religions. This immersion into a culture that seemed so different than my own Christian upbringing actually helped me realize ways to incorporate new very beneficial aspects into my spiritual practice. It was a time of great spiritual development for me, as I spent 3 months trekking from the Amazon down to Lake Titicaca, through the Andes and Machu Picchu to the Colca Canyon. What a time to be alive, and venture to places that many Americans had not yet heard about. Since then I've traveled to many other places in South America where they also use sacred oils for anointing, but I attribute my oil introduction to that first eye-opening adventure. When I returned and researched the topic, I discovered that oils had also been used in Christianity and other religions practiced around the world, and in ancient Middle Eastern cultures since before Christ.

The oil I use most often for anointing comes from a blend of Sandalwood, Frankincense, Myrrh and Rose essentials mixed to fragrant a carrier oil.

OILS I USE

- Rose: Besides unconditional love and purity Rose is one of the Divine Fragrances I speak about toward the end of this book. It's associated with the Mother energy or the Virgin Mary.

- Frankincense: Besides aiding in strength and protection and one of the 3 Gifts to the infant upon his birth, frankincense has a spiritual significance that was more valuable then gold in ancient times and was traded as a commodity.

- Myrrh: Besides assisting in raising vibrational frequency and being a Gift of the Magi, Myrrh is believed to effect the consciousness of the one anointed.

- Sandalwood: Besides the spiritual significance and clearing properties for reducing negativity, it's also associated with the Divine Fragrance of Jesus and with Christ Consciousness or transcendence. Anytime I use sandalwood I feel as if I am being raised upward.

PREPARING OILS FOR FIRST USE

I wanted to share some of my practices when using oils for the first time. In this exercise you will infuse *your* vibrational frequency into the oils. Below are a few steps describing how to prepare the oils for first time use.

1. Take a few minutes to close your eyes and ground yourself. There are instructions on how to do this in the *Preparing the Smudging Facilitator* chapter, if you are not familiar with grounding and centering.

2. Bring all the love of your being into your heart until it feels as if it's overflowing. For those of you who are having trouble with this, think of something that immediately makes you smile and sigh, perhaps a puppy you had when you were a child or a new baby. I'm sure you can think of something.

3. Hold the bottle of oil in your hand and send all that love into the oil.

Now you have your love energy in the oil. This is going to be a wonderful personal anointing oil indeed.

Note:
When I'm cleansing a home, as I move throughout the location, the essence of the oils that I used to anoint myself is present with me in each room of the home, for added cleansing and protection.

ANOINTING YOURSELF

Below is the process to anoint yourself and references to the chapter of this book for corresponding prayers.

1. Take a *tiny bit* of oil and put a drop into your left palm.

2. Spread the oil in your left palm out from the center clockwise using the right index finger, making 3 circles, like the spiral of life symbol.

3. Now take a drop into your right palm and use your left index finger to spread the oil out from the center clockwise 3 times.

The number 3 is significant in many cultures, like for Christians it signifies the trinity; it also resonates with the energies of Ascended Masters and the combination represents the body, mind and spiritual energetic fields around you.

4. Take your palms and join them together, rubbing them clockwise 3 times.

5. Now separate your palms, and in an upward motion breathe in the fragrance and inhale all the energy infused into the anointing oil.

6. Say a <u>Preparation Affirmation /Prayer</u> (when smudging objects or locations) or a <u>Person Anointing Prayer</u> (when working with people or animals) to raise your vibration. You'll find several prayers in the ***Smudging Prayers*** chapter of this book.

10
SMUDGING/CLEANSING CEREMONIES

I use the words smudging and cleansing synonymously because when I experienced forms of smudging in South America, they called it *Limpia*, which means to clean.

Now that you've prepared the space and prepared yourself, you're ready to get to smudging. Below are a few ceremonies to get you started.

COMPLETE LOCATION BLESSING/CLEANSING

It's suggested to perform a full location blessing and cleansing at a minimum of once each season. Some people are very strict and perform this on each solstice and equinox, but I don't think that anyone will haul you off to jail if you perform one a few days before or after. There are several sections in this book that provide information on additional times when a complete ceremony is recommended.

There are separate sections for the major components to be used across ceremonies.

Try and finish the smudging process by ending up at an open exterior door as you come full circle around your location.

Here are the steps for a *Complete Location Blessing/Cleansing*:

Preparation

1. Start with preparing the location. See the chapter titled **Preparing The Location For Smudging** for detailed instructions.

2. Prepare yourself. I've added a chapter titled **Preparing the Smudging Facilitator** that details how to ground and center.

3. If using oils, anoint yourself before beginning the work. Instructions are located in the **Anointing Oils** chapter.

4. Say a <u>Preparation Affirmation Prayer</u> before beginning the work.

Initialization

Part 1

Initialization has 2 parts.

5. Now that you've cleansed and protected yourself, you want to begin with an <u>Initialization Affirmation or Prayer for Self</u>.

The **Smudging Prayer** chapter provides several examples, but you can also use your own. It can be words from a religious book like psalms or a special affirmation of intentions that you feel strongly about. Pick one that resonates with you and say this affirmation to your higher power out loud.

Part 2

6. Face East and light the smudge stick, then fan out the flame so it begins smoldering.

7. Place the smudge stick into the shell. Close your eyes and become one with the smoke, fanning it toward you with

your hand or feather, letting the smoke wash over you.

8. State your intentions to clear the space and make them known to all the energies present in the space by saying an <u>Intention Affirmation or Prayer</u>.

9. Begin in the center of one room. **Note:** Methods include starting at the farthest corner of your location, and finishing at the front door. Another way is to start at the northern most room. I go by layout and move clockwise, so I can finish at an exterior door. Choose the one that works best for your situation.

10. Enter the room and move toward the corner furthest from the room's door.

11. Using the feather/wand, begin the smudging of the room by fanning the smoke against the back wall while saying an <u>Ongoing Smudging</u>

<u>Affirmation/ Prayer </u>out loud with **great intention**.

12. Move clockwise in the room, fanning the smoke outlining every inch of the walls, windows, corners, ceilings and doors within the room. Smudge windows and doors from bottom left, to top left, across from top left to right then top right to bottom right. Remember to smudge inside the closets. After the entire inside of the room is smudged, complete the room by smudging the center of the room. **Note:** Remember to continually say the words you've chosen throughout the process, saying them with strength and love.

13. Toss a pinch of the salt into the middle of the room and on the window sills to purify the room.
Note: If there's a particularly thick lower vibrational frequency in the room, I also sprinkle little pinches of salt around the baseboard.

14. Smudge the door you used to enter the room, both inside and outside, and sprinkle a pinch of the salt in the doorway to complete and seal the room.

15. Continue smudging clockwise throughout the location. Smudge the hallway and move to the next room, until your entire location has been smudged.
    Note: Don't forget about spaces such as the laundry room, garage and basement, if you have them.

Complete the Smudging Ritual

16. When you're finished smudging the entire location, say a <u>Closing Affirmation/Prayer</u> of gratitude outside of the location and complete the ceremony, spreading a little salt at the final threshold.

Final Cleanse of Self

As a practitioner, I suggest that you clear

yourself outside the location after you've completed smudging.

17. Say a <u>Final Cleansing Prayer for Self</u>.

After the smudging is complete, you'll feel a sense of peace, love and light. And who doesn't like that.

QUICK SMUDGE OF A LOCATION

You don't have to go through all the preparation you would for a *Complete Location Blessings/Clearing* for a *Quick Smudge*, but I always do a short self-preparation with a 10 minute meditation to make sure that I'm grounded and centered.

1. If you're using oils, anoint yourself before beginning the work. Instructions are located in the ***Anointing Oils*** chapter.

2. Say a <u>Preparation Affirmation/Prayer.</u>

3. Face East and light the smudge stick, then fan out the flame so the smudge stick is smoldering. Place the smudge

stick into the shell. Close your eyes and become one with the smoke, fanning it toward you with your hand or feather, letting the smoke wash over you.

4. State your intentions to clear the location of negative energy by saying an <u>Intention Affirmation or Prayer</u>.

5. Fan the smoke in the location moving clockwise.

6. When you're finished smudging the area, say a <u>Closing Affirmation/Prayer</u> of gratitude.

7. Finish by saying a <u>Final Cleansing Prayer for Self</u>.

Smudging an Object

Why smudge an object? Think about it. Let's say that you just bought a piece of antique jewelry from a store. It's gorgeous, right, but what you don't see or perhaps don't sense is the energy of the person who probably wore it for years that's still on that piece.

Items that I smudge include pretty much anything you can imagine like jewelry, crystals, cars, boats, items your ex gave you; I think you get the idea. I like to smudge a few objects at a time, but that's just fine if you only have 1 item.

You don't have to go through all the preparation of your space to smudge an object, but I always do a quick self-preparation with a 10 minute meditation to make sure that I'm grounded and centered. Here are the steps to smudge an object:

1. If you're using oils, anoint yourself before beginning the work. Instructions are located in the ***Anointing Oils*** chapter.

2. Say a <u>Preparation Affirmation/Prayer.</u>

3. Light the sage, then wave it so the smudge stick begins to smolder.

4. Close your eyes and let the smoke wash over you.

5. I always state the following as my
    <u>Initialization Affirmation/Prayer</u> when
    cleansing an object or crystal:
    *I am a clear channel of love and light and
    will use this smoke to balance the energy
    of this [object name].*

6. Hold the object in the smoke, turning it
    to ensure that the entire object is
    cleansed. I always state this <u>Smudging
    Prayer</u> when cleansing objects:
    *I cleanse and clear this [object name],
    transmuting any lower vibrational
    energy to love. No longer will it be
    associated with its prior owner.*
    Note: If you're dealing with large
    objects, like An RV, car or boat, you'll
    want to perform a *Quick Smudge*.

SMUDGE YOURSELF

There are times when you want to smudge
yourself. Because I use energy in my line of
work, I'm continually smudging myself.
There are several prayers that I have listed in
the ***Smudging Prayers*** chapter to use
throughout this process.

Here are the steps for smudging yourself.

1. Prepare yourself: Like with smudging a space, you start with preparing yourself. Look at the chapter titled ***Preparing the Smudging Facilitator*** for details on how to ground and center.

2. If using oils, anoint yourself before beginning the work. Instructions are located in the ***Anointing Oils*** chapter.

3. Say a <u>Person Anointing Prayer </u>before beginning the work.

4. Face East and light the sage.

5. Put the smoldering sage into the shell and let the smoke wash over you.

6. Close your eyes and visualize the smoke lifting away all negative energy, thoughts, worries, pain, sadness and heaviness.

7. Say a <u>Prayer for Smudging a Person.</u>

8. Move the shell around and fan the swirls of smoke over every part of your body from head to toe, ensuring that you smudge above the top of your head, the underside of your arms, your underarms, in between your legs, your back (as best you can) and under your feet. Pay attention to the main Chakra areas where you feel there are blockages. This will cleanse your entire energetic body.
    Note: There are practitioners who believe you should start from the head and end at the feet to ensure that all the negative energy goes into the Earth. Others believe that you should end at the head. I don't think there's a wrong way here, as long as you get all of yourself smudged.

9. When complete, say a <u>Closing Affirmation/Prayer</u> of gratitude like this one: *Spirits, thank you for your guidance and strength and for being with me to help raise my vibration and*

release all negative energy from my being.

10. Finish by anointing your forehead in either a cross or spiral of life with a <u>Post Smudge Anointing Prayer</u>. **Note:** A selection of these prayers is located in the **Smudging Prayers** chapter in the <u>Post Smudge Anointing Prayer</u> section.

SMUDGE A PERSON

Below is how to smudge another person.

1. YOU: Prepare yourself. Like with smudging yourself, you start with preparing yourself. Look at the chapter titled **Preparing the Smudging Facilitator** for details on how to ground and center.

2. If using oils, like I do, anoint yourself before beginning the work. Instructions are located in the *Anointing Yourself* section of the **Anointing Oils** chapter.

3. Say the <u>Person Anointing Prayer</u> for yourself.

4. THE PERSON YOU ARE SMUDGING: Have the person you're smudging prepare by taking a few deep breaths. If using oils, have them also anoint themselves using the instructions in the *Anointing Yourself* section of the **Anointing Oils** chapter. Say one of the <u>Person Anointing Prayers</u> found in the **Smudging Prayers** chapter.

5. YOU: Face East and light the sage. Place the smudge stick into the shell. Close your eyes and become one with the smoke, fanning it toward you with your hand or feather, letting the smoke wash over you.

6. Ask the person you're smudging to raise their arms to their shoulders as they stand with their feet shoulder width apart. Stand about 2 feet from the person's body. Have them close their eyes and visualize the smoke

lifting away all the negative energy,
negative thoughts, worries, emotional
pain, sadness and heaviness.

7. Say a <u>Prayer for Smudging a Person</u>
found in the **Smudging Prayers**
chapter, as you move by fanning the
smoke about 3 inches from their body,
from head to toe, ensuring that you
smudge above the top of their head,
the underside of their arms, their
underarms, in between their legs,
their back and under their feet,
cleansing their entire energetic body.

8. Finish by anointing their forehead,
then your forehead with either a cross
or spiral of life with you both saying a
<u>Post Smudge Anointing Prayer</u>.

SMUDGING OUTDOORS

I get asked a lot about smudging outdoors.
When I smudge a location, depending on
what I sense in the space, I may also smudge
the outside perimeter after I complete

smudging indoors. I don't always do that, but if there's a disturbance, I like to be thorough.

Smudging outdoors gives you an opportunity to work with the energy around the house that gets far less attention than the inside of the home.

I've also heard of some practitioners that smudge the property line as well.

FREQUENTLY ASKED QUESTIONS ABOUT SMUDGING

There are many answers to questions about materials located in the **Complete Smudging/Cleansing Toolkit** chapter, but here are a handful regarding the ceremonies.

Is it okay to smudge yourself or do I need to ask a friend. I am just afraid I won't be able to get all of me smudged?
Answer: Although it's easier to have a friend smudge you, it's perfectly okay to smudge yourself. Yes, it may be a little more difficult getting to the back of you, but if you put the

shell behind you and slowly move it up and down your back, then you're cleansing your energetic field.

I am concerned about performing a smudging ceremony with my small children in the home, but I want them to also be cleansed.
Answer: As I point out in a future chapter, for those individuals who have delicate respiratory systems and ailments like asthma, it's best to consult a physician before including them in a ceremony. There are other materials you can use without burning sage.

Can I smudge for a husband?
Answer: The question sparked many an article in my online presence. Although I don't know of any specific smudging ceremonies for getting a husband, I do point you to a few words you can say while smudging your location and yourself that will assist in ridding the energy of the ex-partner.
I ask God and all the heavenly spirits to work with me today to clear this house. Let it free

me from [Your Ex's Name] energy as I release him/her with love. Let this space become a place where my new beloved, my soulmate feels comfortable spending time.

After you finish smudging your space following the instructions I provide about smudging yourself and say the following: *I am only of love and light where I free [Your Ex's Name] energy from my heart, thoughts and spirit.*

It's a good start to releasing the old partner so there's room for a new one.

11

SMUDGING PRAYERS

There are several times during smudging ceremonies where you'll say religious or spiritual prayers and affirmations. They can come from Native American origins, a phrase from a religious book, a spiritual or special affirmation of intentions that you feel strongly about or just something that comes from the heart in that moment.

Below is a collection of prayers divided by where you are within the ceremony. Pick the ones that resonate with you. There are no wrong prayers or affirmations. If you like parts of 2 separate prayers, feel free to combine them in whatever way feels right.

Remember to say these prayers out loud with strength and love in your heart, never with sadness, anger or fear.

AFFIRMATION/PRAYER

paration phase I find that I get
ᵤᵣᵉ energy and protection when I say a
special prayer as I prepare.

After you've taken time to meditate, center,
balance and ground, take time and prepare
yourself. If you're using oils, then as you
anoint yourself recite an affirmation.

Here are several examples:
*I anoint myself with this oil as I ask for my
energy to be only of love, purity and clarity,
with the intention of raising my vibration for
this work.*

*I cleanse and protect myself from all that is
not of the highest vibration of unconditional
love.*

*I cleanse and protect myself in the name of the
Father, Son and Holy Spirit.*

*Oh Great One, clear, center, balance and
protect me in my work.*

Jesus, I ask for your assistance here today and to fill me with your unconditional love.

Mary, my blessed Mother, let your love fill me and bless me in your son's name.

INITIALIZATION AFFIRMATION/PRAYER OF SELF

Before you light the sage or whatever you're burning, most ceremonies ask that you start by standing and facing East, where the sun rises, as a symbol of new beginnings. This is where you'll begin and recite an initialization affirmation or prayer.

Here are several examples:

I ask the Universe to be with me so I may be the perfect channel and help guide and assist me as I clear this space and transmute all that is not love into love.

I ask the Great Spirits to bring forth their medicine and guide me in my work today as I clear this space of all negativity.

I invoke the Light of God to be with me and assist me in being the perfect channel of Love and Light to cleanse this space and all the people in it.

I am a child of God. I ask for the angels to be with me as the perfect channel of love and light to cleanse this space and all people in it.

Create in me a clean heart, O God and put a new and right spirit within me. Be with me as I cleanse this space.

I call upon the great Creator to assist me in my thinking, feelings and actions as I ask for guidance, strength and protection.

Archangel Michael, help me in my work here today and be by my side as my mighty protector.

INTENTION AFFIRMATION/PRAYER

Light the sage or whatever you're burning. This is where you'll recite an intention affirmation or prayer as you face the smoke, allowing it to wash over you.

Here are several examples:
My space is clear, my space is holy, this is a space filled with beauty.

My intention is clear to rid this space of all that is not love.

With this smoke I wash my hands, then wash my face and wash all negativity from this space.

I am a clear channel of love and light and will use this smoke to balance and heal this dwelling.

Negativity that invades this sacred place,
Be gone forever, now leave this space,
You have no hold, no power here,
So heed my words and disappear.
I bring in love and light and grace,
This is the only vibration that fills this space.

Whatever is here invading my space,
If you're not of love,
then leave this place.

All Spirits that fill this hall,
Listen well and listen all.
It's time for you to leave this place,
I ask you to do so with love and grace.

To all spirits, I'm sorry you're lost,
But I am here to help you.
Hear my voice and turn around,
Angels are here to help you on your way.

All spirits trapped in this space, it's time now
for you to embrace the light, without a fight,
And be on your way, this very day.

ONGOING SMUDGING AFFIRMATION/PRAYER
While smudging you will want to move around the space reciting an easy to remember affirmation.

Here are several examples:
Only love and light in this house.

Only energy that is pure love and light and for the highest good in this space.

Only energies that are for the highest vibration of love and light should remain.

This is a house filled with love and light, all negative energy is not welcome here.

Thank you angels for your divine presence as I clear the space for our connection.

God, bless this house.

Only the love of Jesus fill this room.

I bless and cleanse this house in the name of the Father, Son and Holy Spirit.

Jesus, bless this home and rid it of anything that is not of your love.

Note: I always add the following to the end of whatever affirmation I am reciting:
Any energy that is in this house that is not of the highest vibration shall be transmuted to love.

Closing Affirmation/Prayer
I always close a smudging ceremony with a prayer of thanks and gratitude.

Here are several examples:
Mother, Father God, thank you for your

presence with me here today in [name's/my] home as we worked together to raise the vibration and rid the space of all this not pure love.

Father, thank you for sending your saints and angels to work with me to rid this home of all negative energy, replacing it with your love and grace.

Spirits, thank you for your guidance and strength to be with me on this day to cleanse and clear [name's/my] home.

Thank you angels and saints for your presence and help today as we helped lost souls find their way.

Thank you Archangel Michael for your protection and strength as you assisted me in my work here today.

FINAL CLEANSING PRAYER FOR SELF

After the ceremony is complete, I always cleanse myself in the smoke prior to leaving the space and extinguishing the smudge stick. I think that this added prayer affirms my intention to rid myself of any residual energy.

Here are several examples:
I cleanse myself in the name of the Father, Son and Holy Spirit.

I cleanse myself and leave here only with the vibration of pure love.

I transmute any residual energy to pure love, the highest vibration there is.

Person Anointing Prayers
Before I smudge the person, I have <u>them</u> say a prayer as they are using the oil on themselves. This is part of the self-anointing process. They say this prayer after the inhale the fragrant oils that they have spread in the circular motion in their hands.

Here are several examples:
I cleanse and protect myself from all that is not of the highest vibration of unconditional love.

I cleanse and protect myself in the name of the Father, Son and Holy Spirit.

I cleanse and protect myself as I work to rid myself of any and all negativity.

PRAYERS FOR SMUDGING A PERSON
When smudging a person, during the ritual, I usually recite either a popular Native American prayer, but also include additional examples. If I'm smudging myself, I substitute Me and My for You and Your.

Here are several examples:
May your Hands be cleansed, that they create beautiful things.
May your Feet be cleansed, that they might take you where you most need be.
May your Heart be cleansed, that you might hear its messages clearly.
May your Throat be cleansed, that you might speak rightly when words are needed.
May your eyes be cleansed, that you might see the signs and wonders in this world.
May this person be washed clean by the smoke of these fragrant plants,

*And may that same smoke carry your prayers
spiraling to the heavens.*

*May the sun bring you new energy by day,
May the moon softly restore you by night,
May the rain wash away your worries & fears,
May the breeze blow new strength into you,
May you walk gently through the world and
know it's beauty all the days of your life.*

*God, fill this person with only peace and love
as you wash away all that is not of your grace.*

*I ask the universe to cleanse you of all that is
not for your highest good, replacing it with
pure love.*

*I ask the Great Spirits to bring forth their
medicine as I clear [name's/myself] of all
negativity and negative energy.*

POST SMUDGE ANOINTING PRAYERS

After I finish smudging, I always anoint the
person/myself on the forehead. Depending
on the person's beliefs, I will either make the

sign of the cross or I will make the sign of the spiral of life using my thumb and recite one of these two affirmations/prayers.

Here are examples:
Thank you Divine one for cleansing [name/me]. Protect [name/me] from all future energy that is not of the highest vibration of unconditional love.

Jesus, thank you for cleansing [name/me] in your name. Be with [them/me] always blessing and protecting [them/me] with your unconditional love and grace.

12

LIGHTING AND EXTINGUISHING MATERIALS

SAGE AND OTHER PLANTS

Lighting

I get a lot of questions about the best way to light a smudge stick and other dry bundled, wrapped and braided herbs. People are concerned that they may just burst into flames, which is understandable if you've never lit one before.

Actually, when you light a smudge stick it will only flame at the tip. By waving it around it should automatically smolder, causing it to smoke, indicating that it's ready for use.

Note: Lighting sweet grass can take a little longer. Sweet grass should be slightly green when you burn it, so cut off a little at the dry end before lighting.

As you move around the location that you're cleansing, the materials you're using may go out. That's okay, you just want to relight them and continue.

Extinguishing

The easiest way I've found to extinguish a smudge stick is to put it out in a shell or dish containing sand or earth. If sand is not available, then you can also try rolling the lit end in the shell. The key here is to deprive it of oxygen.

As I say this I want you to know that over the past few years I've started to see some pretty large smudge sticks out there. The problem I've experienced with them is that the fire tends to get on the inside, making them harder to extinguish when you're cleansing ceremony is complete. In this instance bigger is not always better and I never use smudge sticks larger than 5-6 inches. I've found that it's easier to have an extra smudge stick with me just in case I need to light another one,, versus going with the larger stick.

PALO SANTO, CEDAR AND OTHER TREES
Lighting

The best way to burn any sacred plant sticks is to ignite the stick and allow it to burn for about 20 seconds to ensure that it has caught fire. Once that is accomplished, wave it out and it's ready for use.

Extinguishing

Putting out barks and sticks is a little easier than sage, pushing them into sand or crushing them into the bottom of your abalone shell or dish.

RESINS
Lighting

The best way to burn resins is to use a charcoal briquette specifically designed to burn resins. Place the briquette in a fire safe dish (suggest iron). If you don't have a fire safe dish, some people have suggested using aluminum foil to line your shell to protect it. Light the charcoal and give it time to burn until it turns white, indicating that it's ready for use. (about 20 minutes), then place the resin on top of the charcoal.

Extinguishing

There is really no easy way that I know of to put out the charcoal once it is lit other than dousing it with water. Doing this will not save the resin that's already burning. For this reason I would suggest the term "less is more" and only use the amount of resin that you want to burn during one session. If you need to add more, you can certainly do so.

WARNINGS

I think it's prudent to point out what may not be obvious to everyone.

- Some people are sensitive to the smoke from herbs. Take care when smudging around infants and small children who have delicate respiratory systems. Always follow the direction of your doctor if someone in the household has allergies, asthma or another forms of respiratory issues.

- Please ensure that the area you are smudging is well ventilated. This is just common sense as well as allowing an escape route for stagnant energy.

- Consult your physician if you're interested in smudging and are pregnant.

- Never leave burning smudge materials unattended and never leave your space until you're sure that these materials are no longer smoldering.

13

BEST TIMES TO SMUDGE

I get a lot of questions about the best times to smudge, whether it's a time of day, a day of the week, time of the month and so on. I know that time is man-made, so there is no bad time to smudge, especially if you feel a shift of energy, but there are specific times I've pointed out below based on the circumstances that I will share with you.

TIME OF DAY

Sunrise

Have you ever heard the words from the song, "It's a new dawn, it's a new day, it's a new life for me." The artist knew what he was talking about as sunrise is when life begins anew. Early morning represents new beginnings, a perfect time to smudge for just that, a new beginning.

Twilight/ Sunset

At the end of light, when darkness falls,

represents the ending of the cycle of the day and a time for letting go of the past.

TIME OF MONTH
Moon Phases

- New Moon (+- 3 days) for new beginnings.

- Full moon (+- 3 days) for releasing and/or letting go.

Using this as a guide, below is when I would smudge based on the event.

To Raise Consciousness/Vibration
There's never a bad time to smudge to raise the consciousness/vibration of person and location.

New Residence
Congratulations on your new residence. The best time to smudge for a new place is after you get settled and preferably during the first moon cycle (30 days) on or about the days surrounding a New Moon in morning.

New Members to Your Household
Person
Whether you're welcoming a new roommate, pet, spouse, baby, etc. once again on or about the days surrounding a New Moon in morning is the best time to smudge.

Belongings
I would take a different tack when it comes to the belongings of the person, since you want to rid them of residual energy. I would smudge these on the Full Moon in the evening.

Life Events
It can get a little tricky with a major life event, but below is a rule of thumb to give you some sound ideas.

- Natural event: You may have just had a hurricane pass through, a time when there's a huge energy upheaval. You survived, so I would smudge as soon as you are able in the morning. It's a new beginning of sorts.

- Losing your job: I'm a glass is half full person and losing a job to me always signifies a new beginning. It's the Universe freeing you up to do something that better resonates with your true self. Most people view this as a loss, and because of that I would smudge the person twice: first in the evening to release any negative emotions about the loss of employment, then again in the morning to embrace the new beginning and new career opportunities that are coming.

- A health condition: I have come to believe that every illness is a manifestation of blocked lower vibrational frequencies, better known as emotions like, fear, worry, resentment, grief and shame. The evening is a better time to smudge when you're not feeling well, to release these emotions from your energetic field as soon as you are able. I would also recommend smudging again on the Full Moon as one of the best times to release

what no longer serves you, even if
you're feeling better.

- Arguments and negative energy: I
  should quiz you here on the best time to
  smudge in this instance, but yes,
  evenings are best. You don't have to
  wait to release those lower vibrations
  (emotions) from your space and person.
  As with the example above, I also
  recommend smudging again on the Full
  Moon as one of the best times to release
  what no longer serves you, even if your
  relationship has improved.

TIME OF YEAR

There are a few times of the year when
smudging is recommended. They fall on the
equinoxes and solstices. The solstices and the
equinoxes are connected with the seasons,
each occurring twice yearly. Many religious
ceremonies are celebrated on these days and
are perfect times to perform a *Complete
Location Blessing/ Cleansing.*

Summer Solstice: June 21
Often called the longest day of the year, it's when the time between Sunrise and Sunset is the longest in the northern hemisphere.

Winter Solstice: December 22
Often called the shortest day of the year, it's when the time between Sunrise and Sunset is the shortest in the northern hemisphere.

Spring Equinox: March 20
Often called the first day of spring, it's when the Sun crosses the Equator moving northward in the northern hemisphere.

Autumn Equinox: September 22
Often called the first day of autumn, it's when the Sun crosses the Equator moving southward in the northern hemisphere.

FREQUENTLY ASKED QUESTIONS ABOUT TIMING
Below are some of the frequently asked questions I get about timing.

How often should I Smudge?
Answer: It depends on the amount of energy in your home. I would suggest smudging whenever you feel lower energies and the situations that I describe in this chapter.

For those not working in energy or healing, I would also suggest a *full house cleansing* at the beginning of each season and a *quick smudge* once a month to keep the energy in your home cleansed and vibrations high.

I smudge my space once a week, but I deal with a lot of different energies in my work, so cleansing is important, especially when you're a channel. And when I'm performing a healing, I perform a *quick smudge* afterward to ensure my energy is now cleared.

Remember, there's never a bad time to cleanse your environment and yourself of old, stale or negative energies. Think of it like showering. You don't *have* to do it every day, but when you do shower, you feel fabulous.

14

DOES DIRECTION MATTER

I've been asked if there's a particular direction to face when beginning a smudging ceremony. If you were attending a Native healing or purification circle, the ceremony would start with the Elder facing East because it's the direction of the rising sun, of new beginnings, coinciding with rebirth.

As do many practitioners believe, I face the East when beginning a smudging ceremony.

Below is information on the elements associated with direction.

OTHER CULTURES AND PRACTICES
- North: Earth
- East: Air
- South: Fire
- West: Water
- Within: Spirit

15

WHEN SHOULD I HIRE A PROFESSIONAL

In writing this book, I know that it would not be complete if I didn't add this chapter about professionals.

If you're dealing with something that you can't handle, then seeking a professional who performs the entire cleansing and smudging ritual is worth every penny, for peace of mind.

There are 3 types of smudging professionals:

1. The pro who'll come and perform a house blessing. Darling, you can certainly bless your house on your own, unless of course you feel more comfortable using a professional. A reputable pro will provide step-by-step instruction as they go through the home and provide you with the tools, so you can continue to smudge your home on your own on a regular basis.

2. The pro who will cleanse your home if you have a disturbance, like Uncle Charlie who's overstayed his welcome. Professionals that will come in and deal with what could be a house full of negative energy and spiritual presences are not cheap, and can cost upwards of $300- $500 for a local pro to come in and cleanse your home and family.

3. Lastly, the pro who'll deal with some of the stuff that Sam and Dean deal with on that unnatural TV show. These pros may or may not deal with attachments to persons, so do your research if you're also dealing with this situation. Someone who can successfully deal with a disturbance of this magnitude and or spiritual attachment will probably charge a lot, so be prepared.

16

BELIEFS, CONTROL AND BLAME

In writing this book, I thought it necessary to add this chapter about beliefs, blame and control.

I receive correspondence from people making statements that I want to rectify. Here are a couple of examples of emails received and my response.

The first email touches on the very topic of beliefs, control and blame that I want to drive home:

I have had problems in our home. I sensed that my oldest step daughter had played with an Ouija board and I found I was right. My oldest step daughter has been back in our house temporarily, and I wonder if she has done something or if something is attached to her.

Folks, please don't blame another person for your own fears. An Ouija board is just a game. It has no power. Don't fall victim to the propaganda in society and Hollywood that's intended to keep us in fear.

I want to stress that beliefs are very powerful, effecting our emotions and our state of being. When I speak to audiences I tell it to them straight.

WHAT YOU BELIEF IS WHAT YOU CREATE

I think it's important to say a few words about control. I want to emphasize that if you walk into someone else's home and the energy feels negative, you can smudge yourself when you get home and tactfully speak to them about smudging, but please don't be adamant telling someone else what they should do. Here's a question I received regarding that very topic.

I would like to know if it's okay to smudge yourself in someone else's home and if it's okay to smudge someone else's homes for them?

Answer: Where you smudge yourself is irrelevant, but it is the right thing to do to seek permission to smudge in someone else's home, prior to doing so. Don't take it upon yourself to invade someone else's space without their consent, whether you feel as if you're doing good or not.

17

What to Do If You Encounter Spiritual Energies

Here's a question from someone recently received:

"Yesterday I did a home smudge for the first time. Afterwards, I felt refreshed, relaxed and my vibration was lifted. I awoke in the middle of the night to the strong smell of sweet incense/herbs. Have you heard of this happening before or do you have any idea why this happened?"

In answering this question I was hesitant to speak about Divine Fragrance, but I will discuss it here as a matter of education.

So, you just smudged your place and you feel amazing. You replaced all stagnant and less than positive energy with only energy that has a higher vibrational frequency. Now you are relaxed and vibrating higher yourself and with that combination of your increased vibration and the increased vibration of your space, you start smelling something wonderful that's not visible. This could be a Divine Fragrance. There are 11 divine fragrances known, each with a corresponding spiritual signature and meaning. For example, they say that the smell of roses signifies unconditional love, exemplified by the Virgin or Great Mother. Sandalwood is likened to Jesus, and Jasmine aligns with compassion and Quan Yin, and a musky smell with manifestation. If you're experiencing an otherworldly scent that doesn't smell like rotten garbage, then you're among good company. I remember when I was in a small town in Brazil, so filled with the grace and love, that I started smelling roses everywhere I went, though no one else I encountered smelled them, and there were no roses to be found. It wasn't until I met up with a new friend, who smiled and verified what I was smelling, explaining to me about Divine Fragrances, did I realize that it was not my imagination.

SOMEONE YOU KNOW

If you're encountering something new and interesting, before you allow your fear to get the best of you, you may just be embarking on a new chapter in your life filled with this new experience.

As I welcome you to my world I want you to know that you're not alone. Actually we're all born with the ability to see behind what some call *the veil*, that layer between our physical reality and what lays beyond. Most people lose that ability as they age. It has to do with something I call the "imaginary focal point" that's learned when we start to reason, at about 4-5 years of age.

I want to help put your fears to rest before panic sets in. Over 95% of the time, it's someone you're close with, like a grandparent, parent, friend, cousin, etc. It could be a person whose energy is related to you, like a relative that passed before your birth. It could be great aunt Sally who died before you met her on this Earth. She was close to your mother and is checking in on you as she has been ever since you were born.

Why haven't you noticed Aunt Sally before?

That is the million dollar question and I have a million dollar answer for you. Without getting into Harmonic Convergences and Concordances, let me just say that there was a significant planetary energy shift that rang in a new age on December 21, 2012. Yes, it marked the end of the Mayan calendar and most people were calling for the end of the world. It was an ending of sorts and a new beginning into a different vibrational frequency for the planet. And with that bell tolling, people's energy also began to shift, now beginning to align to this higher frequency, allowing them to see more of what's behind that *veil.* And that veil has begun to get thin enough for more people to experience these "other things." So before you get out your shotgun or shake in your boots, you may just want to say hello. If you are still and quiet you may just be able to get an idea who has come a knocking. If it is grandma, then tell her that you love her.

And if you decide to smudge, don't worry, you won't chase grandma away, unless of course you specifically ask her to leave.

SPIRIT GUIDES AND OTHER ANGELIC BEINGS
Another possibility is that it's an energy with whom you made an agreement before coming here who promised to provide you with guidance. Many cultures refer to them as Spirit Guides, others call them Guardian Angels. For those who are not aware of this, the word angel actually means messenger, and these energies are perhaps here to provide you with messages and information.

SOMEONE WHO IS LOST
The first time I saw a shadow figure, it was after I moved to Arizona. I was in an apartment that was built on an old homestead. It was then that I met Francis, who was presented as a "shadow figure" that I saw out of the corner of my eye. I kept catching glimpses of him. When friend

Melissa came by, she caught sight of him too. We were sitting out on the balcony and she saw him and commented about it.

"Hey, LeeZa you have a shadow figure in there," she said, as she pointed into the living room.

I was quick to reply, *"I knew there was someone that I was seeing out of the corner of my eye, but never got a full view of him."*

SOMETHING ELSE

If you encounter a presence that you believe is doing you harm, then ask it nicely to leave.

Many people contact me insisting that their home is full of demons that want to hurt and destroy them, so on the outside chance that this is not grandma or Aunt Sally, know that you always have the power to ask that energy to go away. Do it with love and compassion. I want to stress that you don't want to approach any lower vibrational frequency. I explain vibrational frequency in a chapter in this book, but briefly what I mean is do not approach any energy with fear or anger.

I want to point out that if there's a large disturbance like this in your home that if you're not having any luck with kindly asking (with love) that the presence leave, then you are best to call in a professional who deals with these types of disturbances. And make sure you provide them with a full accounting of your situation prior to them coming over, to ensure that they can really handle it. I wrote an article about fakes a while back. No one wants to mess around with something they can't handle, even a phony. Being upfront should weed out the good from the bad.

HOW TO COMMUNICATE WITH SPIRITS

As in the case of Francis, who I talk about earlier in this chapter, we just sat there and spoke to him. We asked if he needed assistance in moving forward and if so, we could ask someone to come help him. He was harmless, just lost and when we asked for help to come show him the way. I never saw him again.

Communicating with energy is not difficult. It's just that people are so afraid when they encounter something new, that their fear gets the better of them and they end up lighting candles and shivering in the corner. When you encounter a spiritual presence, just have a normal conversation with them as if they were physically there with you. Here's a few initial questions you can ask:

> *What's your name?*
> *Why are you here?*
> *How can I help you?*

I also suggest that you get quiet and listen to the answers they may provide. The more open and unafraid you are, the more answers you'll receive. Who knows you may be talking to the spirit of someone really cool.

FREQUENTLY ASKED QUESTIONS ABOUT SPIRITUAL ENERGY

Below are frequently asked questions about Spiritual energy that I have received

I've never smudged to release a spirit to the light. My house sits on a bay in Fenwick Island Delaware. The sunroom literally is standing in the water. Should I be concerned about how water helps empower spirits?

Answer: Yes, water is full of energy and spirits are attracted to areas that are more fluid, but it's about intention and emotion (energy in motion). Your mind has given you concern and only because of how you already feel, I would suggest smudging that area twice, but only because you're already giving that area more power, not because it actually *has* any.

I have something in my house at night. My daughter first told me about this three years ago in her room. It started happening right after my Mom passed. My daughter said that when she was about to fall asleep she would feel something touch her. Is that my mom?

Answer: The timing of the occurrence is certainly very interesting. The only way to be sure is ask. If it is mom, then ask her to show you that it is her in a way that only you would recognize.

18

Some of My Experiences with Energy

With the many experiences that I've had with energy, I want to make a final point to say that there's never anything to be afraid of. This is only energy, whether you want to call it spiritual energy, orbs, spirit guides, angels, etc. When you feel good about yourself, nothing can ever hurt you or lower your vibration. It's only when our emotions and beliefs are based in fear do we allow ourselves to believe that there are bad things going on.

I've cleansed many a space over the years and nothing was ever "bad." What we vibrate we attract in our lives, so maintaining a higher vibration, *love*, is always the best place to be.

Below are just a few examples outside the typical house cleansing and blessings that I have performed, not in any particular order.

My first visit to Abadiânia Brazil was for a couple of months shortly after the beginning of the millennium. If you're not familiar with this place, then let me tell you that there are more for lack of a better term, *energetic beings* there than any other place I've ever visited. I had an experience with a supernatural force that materialized hundreds of pairs of butterflies in an enclosed area in a moment, right in front of me. Okay so this was not the ghost story you were expecting. You see spiritual encounters do not have to be negative.

In a recent visit to Abadiânia Brazil. I stayed in several places while in this sleepy little town, working on my spiritual development. Since I was going to be there for several months, I found long term lodging at a place called the Buddha House, run by a Buddhist nun. As I sat at the long kitchen table speaking to her, what I thought was a cat moved in between the bottom of my legs.

In an instant I knew better, but looked down, stating, *"That better have been a cat."*

"We have no pets here," she replied.

Many people flock to this town for healing and increases in consciousness. I was excited to know that these spiritual entities thought enough of me to say hello in their own way.

When I was married I was very sad at my father-in-law's passing. As we all sat there at his memorial service, someone started to stroke the back of my head. I looked over, thinking that it was my ex-husband. No, it was not anyone of this world.

I will never forget when I was in the audience of a well-known fellow channel from Long Island. As I sat there, although I came alone, that soon changed as I had a spirit with their hand on my left leg and another one with their hand on my shoulder.

Okay, so now for the ghost stories. Yes, I know you are as excited as I am.

I was staying in this old hotel for a month while working a corporate gig. It was clean and comfortable and I loved the historic architecture. Several times when I was in my room, I was experiencing an energy who was smoking a cigar. The smell was distinct in this non-smoking location. I spoke to the manager to find out if that room had any history. Apparently in the 1920's it was a rooming house above a speak easy.

Because I'm sensitive to energy, I'm often in contact with spiritual energy, most making their presence known by touching me, speaking to me, providing me with imagery and information, smells or allowing me to see them. I'll never forget when I was staying in an historic furnished hotel for a few weeks waiting for my new place to be ready. As I was sitting on the toilet, there he was, peeking into the bathroom. I have a rule about times when I am in the bathroom or getting dressed and quickly made it known that it was not an appropriate time for him to visit.

A friend called me stating that her niece had moved into a new house with her family. She said that there was something strange going on with an object that she had on a top shelve in her kitchen. She was perplexed because it kept turning around. I explained that moving objects is not uncommon when dealing with spirits, but she was freaked out. I made sure to bring along my tool kit when I visited her family at Thanksgiving. What we were able to surmise after I came over to visit and help her communicate with this energy, it was just her grandmother trying to get her attention. The item on the top shelf was something that granny gave to her years earlier.

Some people like having spirits around, at least old hotel owners do. I laugh as I recall the time when I was in a spirit filled boutique hotel built in the 1930's in Reno, and asked to visit the place before the paranormal investigators came with all their equipment and cameras.

As I walked into the hotel, I could feel that it was filled with residual energy. I commented as we walked up to the 2nd floor balcony that there was a lady there who likes to hang out in this space.

When the paranormal investigators who visited a week later pointed out to the manager about a large energy spike on the 2nd floor balcony, the manager turned and said, *"Yes, we know, LeeZa Donatella was here last week and told us about the woman who likes to stay in this area."*

The manager quickly called me and told me they had arrived. I'd never seen a true paranormal investigator outside a TV show, so I jumped in the car to check it out. They had set up their equipment down the basement where there was thought to be a lot of activity.

The long fluorescent lights were switched off, so the manager and I joined hands as we made our way down the stairs. The investigators were in the back room, but their computer was set up near the far doorway.

We carefully walked hand-in-hand to look at the screen. It was then that the lights sizzled. First for a second, then for over 5 seconds. I was impressed knowing that the energetic being was trying to get our attention. The manager however, petrified, squeezed my hand to the point of causing me extreme pain. I leaned in and said 3 words to her,

"Oh honey, it's only energy."

When the energetic spirit started to touch me, a feeling similar to being poked in the back, I simply replied, *"I know you're here buddy, but you don't have my permission to touch me. Besides, the shows in the other room."*

Remember, when you show no fear, then fear will never get the best of you.

I would like to leave you with a final thought.

**Nothing has power over you
unless you allow it.**

I believe that fear is our only enemy here. *Vibrating Love* is the key to a happy life and higher vibrational frequency and energetic field.

If all of a sudden you experience something that is new, like spiritual energy, say hello and ask its name.

Welcome to my world!

CPSIA information can be obtained
at www.ICGtesting.com
Printed in the USA
FSHW01n1956260718
50941FS